CW01431597

Translations From Heinrich Heine's Buch Der Lieder

TRANSLATIONS
FROM
HEINRICH HEINE'S
BUCH DER LIEDER.

BY EMIL A. C. KEPPLER.

C. H. PEASE,
CANAAN, CONN.
1901.

to Prof. Price, with cordial regard; and since thanks for his encouragement and guidance,

Emil Keppler

Oct 18/1901.

TRANSLATIONS
FROM
HEINRICH HEINE'S
BUCH DER LIEDER.

BY EMIL A. C. KEPPLER.

C. H. Pease, Printer,
CANAAN, CONN.
1901.

213367

PRICE LIBRARY

Copyrighted, 1901,
by
EMIL A. C. KEPPLER.

UNIVERSITY
OF VIRGINIA

TO H. B. A.

Love is the theme of story,
  Of sacrifice and song;
And of its crown of glory,
  Joined to its cowl of wrong,
Heine of all its singers
  Is foremost amongst the throng.

I, with my trembling fingers,
  Follow his song-burst strong,
That floods the hearts of mortals,
  Sweeping them swift along
Sunbeams from heaven's portals,—
  Lo! At thy feet his song.

                                    E. K.

Twin Lakes, Conn., July 15, 1901.

CONTENTS.

6

THOU, WHO ART SO PURE AND FAIR.

(Die Du Bist So Hold Und Rein.)

———

Thou, who art so pure and fair,
Maiden, joyous, debonaire,
To thy service everywhere
Would my life alone I swear.

Thy sweet eyes, with lustre rare,
Gleam like moonlight through the air;
Rosy tints of roses fair
Strew thy red cheeks here and there.

And from out thy small mouth there,
Rows of pearls peep everywhere;
But of gems the one most rare
Thy pure bosom guards with care.

Love, where reverence hath share,
May be, thrilled my heart with care,
When I first beheld thee there,
Maiden, joyous, debonaire.

LET ME WITH MY LOVED ONE BE.

(Wenn Ich Bei Meiner Liebsten Bin.)

———————

Let me with my loved one be,
   My heart then waxeth proud;
Then riches fill my treasury;
   I cry earth's sale aloud.

But when the parting hour draws near,
   To leave her swan white arms;
Then all my riches disappear
   And I must beg for alms.

JUST AT DAWN I WAKE AND QUERY.

(*Morgens Steh' Ich Auf Und Frage.*)

Just at dawn I wake and query,
 " Will she come to-day? "
Just at dusk I sigh aweary,
 " Absent, too, to-day."

Through the night, by cares encumbered,
 Sleeplessly I lie;
Dreaming, as if half I slumbered,
 In the day I wander by.

SWEET LOVE, PLACE THY HAND ON THAT HEART OF MINE.

(*Lieb, Liebchen Leg's Hændchen.*)

Sweet love, place thy hand on that heart of mine,
Dost hear, in its chamber the smiting fine?
A carpenter works there, ill natured and sly,
Who builds me a coffin wherein to lie.

There's hammering and beating by night and by
      day.
Long since, it has driven my sleep away;
"Sir Carpenter, speed and hasten thee,
That I may soon asleeping be."

I WISH THAT ALL MY LYRICS.

(Ich Wollte Meine Lieder.)

———————

I wish that all my lyrics
  Were flowers sweet and fine;
I'd send them for their fragrance
  Straight to that love of mine.

I wish that all my lyrics
  Might only kisses be;
In secret would I send them
  To kiss her cheek for me.

I wish that all my lyrics
  Were tiny, little peas;
I'd brew and stew a pea soup
  That would the palate please.

FIRST I FELT I MUST DESPAIR.

(Anfangs Wollt' Ich Fast Verzagen.)

First I felt I must despair,
    Could not bear it then or now,
Yet I bore it, and still bear,—
    If you love me, ask not how.

13

YONDER WHERE THE STARS ARE GLOWING.

(Oben, Wo Die Sterne Gluehen.)

Yonder where the stars are glowing
We must find those pleasures flowing
Which we were denied below;
Only in death's cold arms folded
Can all life with warmth be moulded,—
And the night to day's light grow.

WHENE'ER YOUNG HEARTS ARE BREAKING.

(Wenn Junge Herzen Brechen.)

When'eer young hearts are breaking,
  The stars show smiling faces;
They say, while merry making,
  Upon their far, blue spaces:

"Though wretched men love truly,
  Their hearts with love o'erloaded,
They vex themselves unduly,
  And unto death are goaded.

"That love did never know us,
  Whose bane they cannot sever,
Those wretched men below us,—
  Hence, too, we live forever."

I'LL REVEL IN JOY OF WOODLAND GREEN.

(Ich Will Mich Im Gruenen Wald Ergehn.)

I'll revel in joy of woodland green,
Where flowers bud and the birds are singing,
For, let there but once be a grave to hold me,
From sight and sound the earth shall fold me,
The growing flowers I cannot glean,
My ears will not hear bird songs aringing.

OH, THOU KNEWEST COOK AND KITCHEN.

(*O, Du Wusstest Koch Und Kueche.*)

Oh, thou knewest cook and kitchen,
  Nook and cranny, gate and door,
Ever when we strove together
  Thou wert always there before.

Now thou art to wed my sweetheart,
  Friend, I can't put up with that;
Still more madd'ning is that you I
  Must congratulate thereat.

ALL THEIR HEARTS ARE FILLED WITH YEARNING.

(*Allen Thut Es Weh Im Herzen.*)

All their hearts are filled with yearning
　Who behold the youth palefaced;
For whom sorrow, heart ache's burning,
　On his face deep furrows traced.

Sympathetic breezes proffer
　Cooling to his heated brow;
Cheer unto his heart there offer
　Smiling maidens—coy till now.

From the townsmen's noisy bustling
　Hies he to the greenwood shade,
Gaily there the leaves are rustling,
　Songs of birds ring through the glade.

But the singing soon is ended,
　Sadly rustle leaf and tree;
When the sad-souled youth has wended
　His slow way, oh, wood to thee!

GOOD SQUIRE, ARISE, AND SADDLE QUICK.

(*Die Botschaft.*)

Good squire, arise, and saddle quick,
    And mount thy steed apace,
And scurry through both wood and field
    To Duncan's royal place.

There, stealing to the stable, wait
    Till thee the groom hath spied,
Then ask, "Of Duncan's daughters which
    May be the promised bride?"

And if he say, "The dark one 'tis,"
    Then bring me word with speed;
But if he say, "The blonde one 'tis,"
    For hurry there's less need.

Go, call on master Roper, then,
    And buy a rope for me;
And slowly ride, say not a word,
    And bring it home with thee.

'TWAS IN THE WONDROUS MONTH OF MAY.

(Im Wunderschoenen Monat Mai.)

'Twas in the wondrous month of May,
  When buds with bloom were showered,
Forthwith within my bosom
  Love blossomed out and flowered.

'Twas in the wondrous month of May,
  When all birds sang in choir,
I uttered there before her
  My yearning and desire.

AMID MY TEARS UPSPRINGING.

(Aus Meinen Thrænen Spriessen.)

———

Amid my tears upspringing
   Full many sweet flowerets throng,
And all my sighs are turning
   To nightingales in song.

And if thou dost love me, dearest,
   Take thou the flowerets all,
And under thy window shall echo
   The nightingale's sad call.

WHENE'ER I LOOK INTO THINE EYE.

(Wenn Ich In Deine Augen Seh.)

———————

Whene'er I look into thine eye
Then all my woe and pain pass by;
But when I kiss thy lips with mine,
I grow right well and feel right fine.

Whene'er I lean upon thy breast
With glow of heavenly joy I'm blessed.
But when thou sayest, "I love thee,"
Then must I weep, ah, bitterly.

ALL MOTIONLESS AND FIXED.

(Es Stehen Unbeweglich.)

All motionless and fixed
  The stars have stood above,
For thousands of years exchanging
  Their looks of plaintive love.

They serve them of a language,
  So rich in beauty's blend,
Yet not a master linguist
  This tongue can comprehend.

But I have mastered and learnt it,
  And nought can this knowledge displace,—
There served me for a grammar
  My heart's best beloved's sweet face.

I HATE THEE NOT; AND THOUGH MY HEART DOTH BLEED.

(Ich Grolle Nicht.)

I hate thee not; and though my heart doth bleed,
Love, lost for aye, I hate thee not indeed.
Howe'er with diamonds thou be bedight,
There falls no gleam into thy bosom's night.

Long know I this. I saw thee in a dream;
And in thy heart, I saw, the night supreme,
And saw the snake that feeds upon thy heart,
I saw, my love, how full of woe thou art.

AYE, THOU ART WRETCHED, NOR DO I COMPLAIN.

(*Ja, Du Bist Elend, Und Ich Grolle Nicht.*)

Aye, thou art wretched, nor do I complain,
  My love, we two are doomed to wretchedness;
Until death break our wounded hearts in twain,
  My love, we two are doomed to wretchedness.

I see the scorn that on thy lip doth rest
  And see thine eye blaze forth defiantly
And see the pride that swelleth up thy breast,—
  Still art thou wretched—wretched e'en as I.

Thy lips an unseen agony surrounds,
  From unseen tears thine eyes grow lustreless;
Thy haughty bosom nurtures secret wounds,—
  My love, we two are doomed to wretchedness.

THERE'S FLUTE AND VIOLIN PLAYING.

(Das Ist Ein Flœten Und Geigen.)

———

There's flute and violin playing
  And trumpet's burst of sound;
Midst bridal measures swaying
  My heart's best beloved is found.

What endless clanging and droning
  Of drum and pipe of reed;
Throughout are sobbing and moaning
  Good angels at my need.

BEAUTEOUS, BRILLIANT, GOLDEN STAR.

(Schœne, Helle, Goldene Sterne.)

Beauteous, brilliant, golden star,
Greet my loved one now afar;
Say, I'm still, as once she knew,
Ill at heart, and wan and true.

IN AGONY AND ANGUISH.

(Aus Meinen Grossen Schmerzen.)

In agony and anguish
My tiny songs I utter;
On sounding, bright pinions they flutter
To where my beloved doth languish.

They flew to my loved one's bosom;
But homeward returned with lamenting,—
Lamenting yet never commenting
On what they beheld in her bosom.

THE HEAT OF SUMMER RESTETH.

(Es Liegt Der Heisse Sommer.)

The heat of summer resteth
　Upon thy cheeks divine,
The frost of the winter resteth
　Within that heart of thine.

All that is sure to alter,
　Thou precious love of mine,
Thy cheek shall glow with winter,
　With summer that heart of thine.

29

ALL POISONED ARE MY LYRICS.

(*Vergiftet Sind Meine Lieder.*)

All poisoned are my lyrics—
  How other could it be?
For poisonous draught was poured
  Into my life by thee.

All poisoned are my lyrics—
  How other could it be?
I bear many snakes in my bosom
  And thee, oh, sweetheart—thee!

I LAY IN DREAMS AWEEPING.

(Ich Hab' Im Traum Geweinet.)

I lay in dreams aweeping,
   I dreamt of thee in the grave;
I wakened and the tear drops
   Still to my eyelids clave.

I lay in dreams aweeping,
   I dreamt thou desertedst me,
I wakened and I wept then
   A long while bitterly.

I lay in dreams aweeping,
   I dreamt thou wert true to me,
I wakened, and still there were streaming
   Tears on my tear drop sea.

A STAR DESCENDETH DOWNWARD.

(*Es Fællt Ein Stern Herunter.*)

———————

A star descendeth downward
  From out its glittering height,
That is the star of passion
  That falls there in my sight.

There fall from the apple branches
  Full many a leaf and bud;
There come the ironical breezes
  And play as they onward scud.

The swan sings on the mill pond
  And paddles up and down,
And ever softer singing,
  Into the waves goes down.

It is so still and darksome,
  All scattered leaf and flower,
The star with crackling exploded,
  The swan song has lost its power.

AT THE CROSSROADS THERE LIES BURIED.

(Am Kreuzweg Liegt Begraben.)

At the crossroads there lies buried
   Who perished by suicide;
There flowers a sky blue blossom—
   The plant called Beggar's Pride.

I stood and sighed at the crossroads,
   The night was cold and still;
There waved in the moonshine sedately
   The Beggar's Pride at will.

ON MY FAR TOO GLOOMY PATHWAY.

(In Mein Gar Zu Dunkles Leben.)

On my far too gloomy pathway
  Fell one day a vision sweet;
Now that my sweet vision faded,
  Wraps me round night's sable sheet.

Children playing in the darkness,
  Feel their joyous spirits wane;
And, to drive away their terror,
  Sing their very loudest strain.

I, a mad cap youth, am singing
  Just this moment in the dark,
Though my song may not sound joyous,
  From my fear it freed me, mark.

I ROAM THE WOODLAND AWEEPING.

(Im Walde Wand'le Ich Und Weine.)

I roam the woodland aweeping,
  The thrush is sitting on high;
She hops and sings apeeping,
  "What woe on thee doth lie?"

The swallows, thy relations,
  Could tell thee, child, if they chose,
They dwelt in knowing stations
  Where sweetheart's windows rose.

AH, DEATH, IT IS THE COOLING NIGHT.

(Der Tod, Das Ist Die Kuehle Nacht.)

Ah, death—it is the cooling night,
    And life—it is the sultry day,
    The dusk doth come, I'm drowsy,
The day hath worn me weary quite.

Over my bed there riseth a tree,
    The youthful nightingale sings there;
    She sings of nought but loving,
E'en dreaming, her songs haunt me.

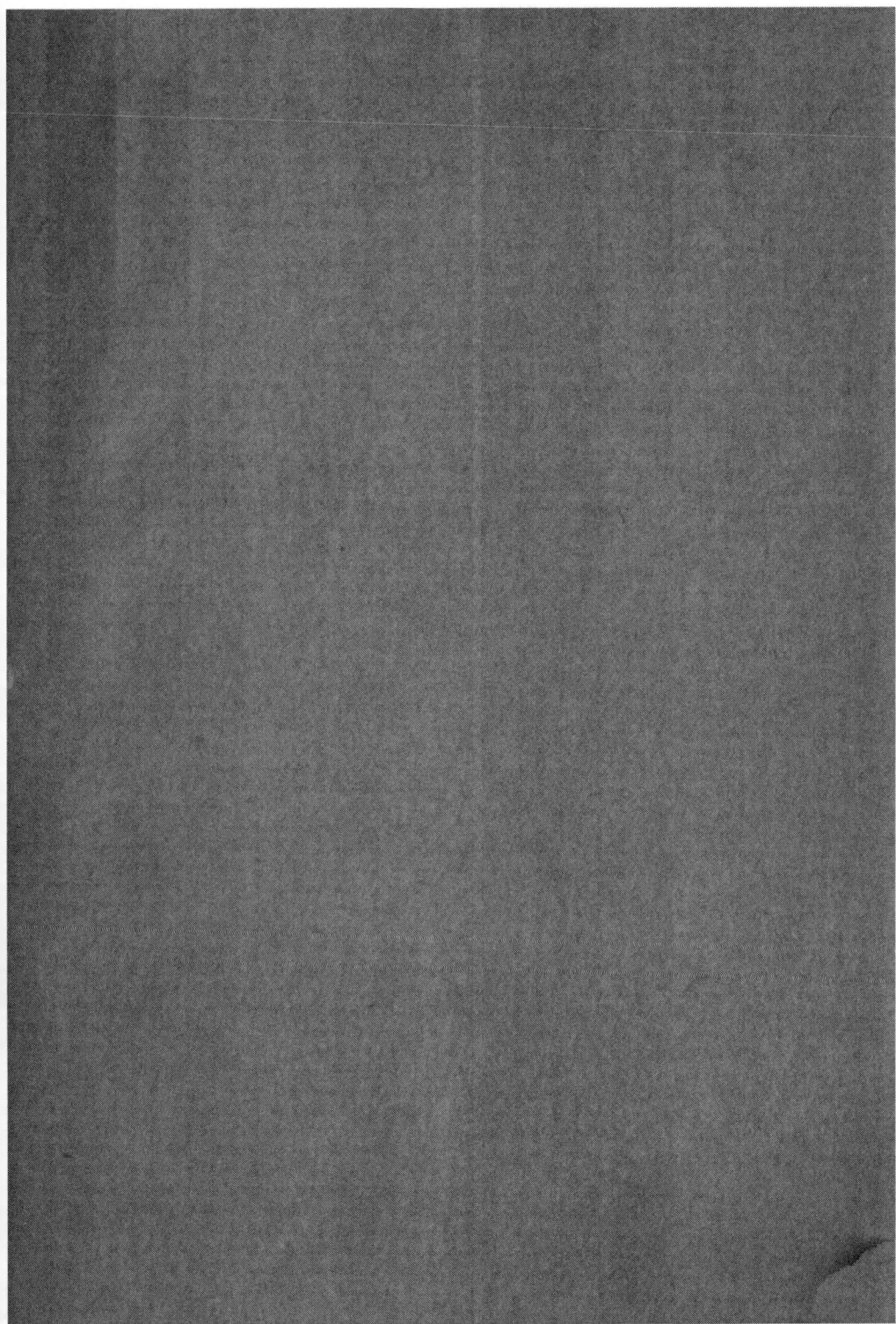

ALDERMAN LIBRARY
The return of this book is due on the date
indicated below

DUE	DUE
~~APR 19 1948~~	

Usually books are lent out for two weeks, but
there are exceptions and the borrower should
note carefully the date stamped above. Fines
are charged for over-due books at the rate of
five cents a day; for reserved books there are
special rates and regulations. Books must be
presented at the desk if renewal is desired.

Ingram Content Group UK Ltd.
Milton Keynes UK
UKHW020106090323
418239UK00006B/563

9 781378 505892